WE HAVE THE MELON

We Have the Melon

Gregory Woods

CARCANET

First published in 1992 by
Carcanet Press Limited
208-212 Corn Exchange Buildings
Manchester M4 3BQ

A CIP catalogue record of this book is
available from the British Library.
ISBN 0 85635 966 1

The publisher acknowledges financial assistance
from the Arts Council of Great Britain

Set in 10pt Garamond Simoncini by Bryan Williamson, Darwen
Printed and bound in England by SRP Ltd, Exeter

In memory of
Nicholas Green
(1954-1989)

Acknowledgements

I want to thank Stephen Spender and William Scammell for their help and encouragement at crucial stages in the preparation of this book.

Some of the poems were first published in the following magazines: *Gehenna, The Great Imbroglio, PN Review, Quartz, Rock Drill, Square Peg* and *Stand*; and in the Oscars Press anthology *Take Any Train*, edited by Peter Daniels. Other poems appeared in Practical Criticism exams at the University of Salerno, 1980-1984. 'First of May' was a prize-winner in the 1989 Skoob/*Index on Censorship* poetry competition.

Contents

PART ONE

Roughly Speaking

The sky was matador
to a snorting night.
One by one in the breeze

our smiles flickered out.
The photographer
veiled like a widow

dabbed at his monocle.
We witnessed spellbound
flex of calves and arse

as he conjured out of his
maddening cape a blade
like a confident handshake.

This is the way I
remember word for word
roughly speaking my

boyhood whenever a storm
slashes the blackout
and inflicts on some

demented oak, like it
or not, electro-
convulsive therapy.

Africa my boyhood
and none of my business,
where do I belong?

To placate lovers who
demand a life story
I offer my lasting

sun-tan, souvenir
of ant hills, laterite
and corrugated iron.

I dip into ivory
stoups to cross myself
with their albino sperm.

Puberty was roused from
sleep by realistic
apparitions. Hair

began to dart through
your skin like the coils
of old mattresses.

A first-year was yelling
Catullus into a knot
of discarded pyjamas:

deaf to the chapel bell,
he spurted a dactyl
into wet flannel.

Weeks before the beard,
with the body bared
on the cherub's bed

still a perfect bud,
so proud of his bowed
genitals that bode

sweetly for a bride
or the boy ill-bred
enough to beat her bid,

how could he be bored
with the time he must bide
before turning bad?

After Sunday lunch
the breaking voices
of a solitary world

close family doors
behind them and go
kicking cans to blazes.

Their paths intersect
but they never meet.
They can hear each other

keen in the empty
streets, adam's apples
reckless with restraint.

Over the Wall

Scale the trunk. Straddle a thick limb. Already gold-leafed
    By summer afternoons, he thinks he's unseen in his walled
Garden of immaculate lawn. Give your pal a hand: lift
    Him to your vantage on the naked man's fanatic world.
      But leave all your threatening laughter unlaughed.

Clench yourselves silent. Don't allow a cough or reflex kick
    To warn him. Drain your brains thoughtless, as if left
Lobe had cancelled right. Even when he turns to cook
    His front, don't react. Record of the weeks he's loafed
      Alone here, his skin (colour of cork

Drawn from red wine) looks even from this distance wet
    With sweat. Grass cuttings stick to his chest and cock
As though his hairs were green. No patch of white
    Allures the eye. Like a wooden statue stained to caulk
      It against weathering, he has the wit

To seem changeless for a while. Think of nothing, boys,
    Say less. Stay where you are. Wait for the weight
Of your swelling into ripeness to bend your boughs
    To touch the earth. Or wait at least till what
      You see or fancy of him bores

You to death. Look. A wet gesture nears the broad
    Interval between his tits: drawing-pins securing him to baize.
He tries unpinning one; it resists. In the thick braid
    Of his cock a knotted pulse unravels, and he bares
      His breath to a flurry of bread

In the air, sole host and guest at this feast
    On his own embodied stink. If the breeze itself, brewed
Thick to a broth on his sullen flame, is the first
    To savour him, you boys come close behind. You brood
      On breath, spun giddy, like sailors forced

To swallow their beloved, killing sea. The walled garden's heat
    Wells up and overflows, scorching your beech. You cling fast
To its bark and hug the peril of its height
    As if only danger can save you from a fist
        The day has flexed for the hit.

Whatever happens, don't close your eyes. For both your sakes,
    Suppress vertigo, cramp, need to urinate, etc. If a hot
Pinch of cotton should tease your loins, or your socks
    Ruck between the toes, concentrate: not on any trivial hurt
        Of yours, but on him who seeks,

Among the yesses of those who desire him, a no.
    For he comes here to hear nothing of the sex
They decide he represents. He bares his body to ignore
    It, as if clothing alone made it visible, and psychs
        Himself up into the apathy of Noah.

You're watching the suitor who's managed to book a tryst
    With himself. No one is late, the appointment is now,
He has built up what amounts to a complete trust
    In himself: by representing his own past and pastures new,
        He aims to vanish without being traced.

But you can still see him. Look. There's no doubt:
    The shape of him is, while there's grass to contrast
Him with, body enough for the shortest-sighted to date
    Or dote on, no less solidly exposed than if trussed
        Up with buck-skin and given dirt

To eat by the peerless one who calls him bitch;
    As manifest as though publicly stripped to pay the debt
Of an assumed humility, yet all the more securely butch
    For seeming a target as open to love's contingent dart
        As to the kisses of the birch.

You can see him. But be warned. Wasn't it Freud
    Who said life can't be rendered faultless once you botch
It? Is it any wonder if your nerves are frayed
    And if even in the soaring fastness of your beech
        You start to quiver like leaves, afraid

Not only now of being sighted, but of getting enticed
　　　Into restraints from which only the dead are ever freed?
He will contrive by remote control to shape your taste,
　　　Attentive to the detail of your dreams, sealing a fraud
　　　　　You won't admit to, let alone contest.

Why not conspire with him to have his body banned
　　　From sight? Save us from this basted, brown-as-toast
And tasty feast his idle rigour has prepared, small boned
　　　For modesty of stature, but built like a trapeze artiste
　　　　　For catching falling boys. Before the bond

His beauty swears you to has time to tighten, spurn
　　　This yearning: for if you let his parasitic body bind
You to it, if only across the long suspended span
　　　Of your gaze, it will surely compel you to bend
　　　　　The steadfast branch of your spine,

And you will find your 'apples' well and truly 'cored'...
　　　So look – but don't be taken in. Should he spawn
What seems a future for you, as if he cared
　　　A toss for your welfare, offering the castles in Spain
　　　　　His nipples constitute or the tensed cord

Of his stomach to your gullible touch, sooner or later
　　　You'll see you have nothing to gain from what's occurred
Between his active indifference and your desire: for the latter
　　　(The infection he passes you while wishing you already cured)
　　　　　Could partake of him by the litre

Without once detecting a drop of spirit in the blend.
　　　He has already dropped the likes of you, like litter,
Whether short or tall, pliable or hard to handle, blond
　　　Or dark, as if just to make his pockets lighter.
　　　　　Although no fool, he's all but blind

To the degrees of beauty or to lovers unusually skilled,
　　　Inventive, athletic, vicious and so on; even to the ballooned
Laps of the well-endowed. Why, you'd have to scald
　　　His foreskin to convince him you were any less bland
　　　　　Than he is. He wants you schooled,

If he wants you at all, by the obscure books
    Of distance. He wants to be not smiled but scowled
At, not followed but to see you turn your backs
    On him by way of a snub. (If having scaled
        Your tree you'd stretched your famished beaks

To take the worms of yearning, he might have passed
    It off as yawning and been charmed.) Still he bakes
And still you look. Why bother to desert your post
    And scramble back down to where you left your bikes
        For a quick flit into the past?

This has been a day from which you can't regress
    So fast. No matter how tenaciously your lips are pursed
As you go home, nor how eagerly you grease
    Them with supper, there's now no ducking what you've pieced
        Together about bum-boys in ancient Greece:

Pleasure, beauty, balance, form! Look, the very arses you sit
    On denounce you, implicating you as accessories to the grace
He withholds from you. You're as involved in the sight
    Of his cock as if you were flattening the grass
        Beside him. Who you are, what sort

Of outcomes have been chosen for you as your goal
    In life, bear no relation to what you once sought
For yourselves. Your heroes have been ousted by a ghoul,
    Ideals by obsession. All of your nights are now set
        In a garden stirred by a gale.

But you'll never shiver here, not even naked, never here:
    For I'm the viewer of voyeurs. Listen, it's my guile
And not the breeze that whispers in your hair,
    My breath that keeps you warm. Mine is the gall
        That gurgles in the voice you hear.

Your belief that I'm in league with *him* is based
    On the convincing fear that I might want to hire
For a night whichever one of you he judges best.
    Isn't that why I pitch my voice a fraction higher –
        To suit the beauty in the beast?

But I've no time for him. Half a lifetime whiled
    Away in the sullen company of lads with boasts embossed
On chests expanded for desire – and still we fail to weld
    Together at the point where lust ignites its pallid burst.
        Do you wonder the nights are wild?

Although I tuned to something true when you two wailed,
    Your quarry's moans were not so much spontaneous as willed.
When he yawned, tears or what pass for them welled
    Into his eyes. The first dead leaves of autumn whirled
        Across a tanning lawn no longer walled.

Adolescent summers
lapse in a quiver
of odorous fingers.

Fevers seething within
the blistered hollows
of hooligans' fists

infect the loveless
schoolboys of the world
with deepest sleeplessness.

May they be wrestled
into submission by
their brawny pillows!

The fullback comes in
from the playing field
with mud on his thighs.

He commits himself
to the shower's veil
and bouquet of suds

(nothing touches him
but this modesty)
and relinquishes

the mud on his thighs
like stockings furling
under their own weight.

The last of the away team
was happy to show off
to three spellbound juniors

his up-to-the-minute
black nylon underpants
inches from our eyes.

Like a conjuror's hat
they contained far more than
they looked as if they could.

I spent half that night
making more and more
magic in my lap.

'A Child is Being Beaten'

Come, let
us establish
order. In a Queen Anne house, poised

beside
the subdued lawns,
a sense of proportion is taught.

Order
is compacted
with a handshake behind baize doors,

man to
man, no blubbing.
Bruises deepen in the mirror,

fingers,
touchy fingers,
they sting on corrugated flesh.

Over
one shoulder the
glass catches light in a friend's eye.

A quick,
unfunny joke
declares as little as he dares

but means
between the lines
far more than either bargained for.

Get into
bed, lights out,
no talking. Under a fading

chirrup
of bedsprings, the
air is infested with coiled socks.

The words
in last whispers
evaporate into pure breath.

All's quiet,
reason prevails,
balance, cool-heartedness, respect...

Only
in nightmare, lust
spits froth on human carrion.

Nothing justifies
the sentimental
madness of my teens:

believing the world
runs on rational
principles! But insane

consolations turned
up, like a taste for
the curding moisture

of *mozzarella*,
little white bottoms
in little white shorts.

Ganymede grows up.
Lips embittered by
the lees of service

purse on a silent
declension of plosives,
curses he lets out

after he leaves you
as if breaking wind.
Every smile is moulding

kisses that poison
while his suppressed voice
thickens like his cock.

PART TWO

He turned the key, closed
the window, drew the blind,
draped pants over the prying

keyhole. The other put on
the radio to drown
any sound they might make.

Then the tall one, the one
who had asked if the
receptionist was to be

trusted, switched off the
light and they made good
their burial alive.

At nightfall, when lack
deepens faith in luck,
the businessmen lurk

to taste their own laic
frankincense of luke-
warm piss. Over a lake

all the cisterns leak
into, their eyes lock
on a meaning look.

Commerce, as they lick
their lips, arises like
a complicated lark.

All night the plywood
walls are sprouting hard-ons
like sudden mushrooms.

The sleepless connoisseur
collects and eats them
fresh, unseasoned, raw.

His appetite lasts,
intact, until the sun
and larksong emerge

from the lock-up like
a boy's mouth reciting
measures of thick sperm.

The straitlaced fister
takes a puppet-master's
view, putting you on

like new opera gloves,
attentive to his nails
lest he ladder you.

Hoodwinked by his own
vanity, he consults
you like a wrist-watch

as if expecting
something to happen
that isn't going to.

Through the glory hole
a world contrives itself
of such integrity

as leaves no surfeit
of doubt or torpor
to its own geometry.

Nothing that happens
here happens by chance
and nothing goes wrong.

Phallus, circle, mouth
combine one purpose,
one physique, one act.

Livery

I do not know how
to strip you, short of
skinning you alive.

You wear your bareness
neatly pressed, as if
the deftest touch will

crumple it. But scar
me for life with the
gauntlets of your strength.

Lapping your waist,
an intended belt-print
impedes my headway.

Even your groin is
haunted by the faint
outline of a pair

of shorts. I maul their
fabric, in the vain
hope that it will give.

And when I call for
help, scorched on the hot-
plate moon, you dress my

wounds in unlikely
dreams, of hidebound men.
Breathless, mummified.

Recrimination

I've slept with you a million times.
I can remember only one.
We ached as if it were the last.
But we had only just begun.
Our kisses came to light like crimes

which we were sentenced to repeat.
Every embrace was an assault.
Our first night should have been the last.
It set the pattern to our fault.
Now when we split the spoils we cheat.

Abraham

The beaver does not stay his decision.
With teeth stropped on native carpentry
He arms the routine ablution and lops
His balls. A ransom for the dogs.

Call off your romance. I have sentenced
My sacrifice to the tangle of your
Lap. The dawn will do the rest
With its kerosene and box of Swans.

I once fed you on
bean sprouts and watched them
emerge the next day

unassimilated
but all the richer for
their mellow odyssey.

I have followed their
route on apocryphal
charts, absent in you

like a friend who vanishes
for months and reappears
instructed, satisfied.

The Visitor

He arrives seldom like hopes
we are silent like the dead
he lays me out like a corpse

he lies on me like a lid.

The philosopher's
unseen table was never
so in need of proof.

Even your stillnesses
are performed, your silence
the running comment on

whichever theory
of beauty you embody.
Torso genitals lips

you, without your claque
the ugly, would not have been
so much as thought of.

Enough of this chatter.
Leave your political
opinions and vague

aspirations behind.
Come to bed. I want
to know how you taste

but not your tastes,
how you feel but not
what pass for feelings.

I crave nothing but
to hold forth with your
articulate flesh.

When he spread himself
like that, looking back
at me with a grin

intended to dement,
I was never less
inclined to madness.

I entered him as
Alice or Aladdin
entered fantasy,

my passion rational
as splitting the atom
or spaying the cat.

I purloined the pleasures
greedy children find
in mere honeypots,

light-fingered between
the pale haunches of
an eighteen-year-old.

Flaunting his lavish
glamour, he scattered
unforeseen largesse

of silver, his hole
convulsed like the drawstrings
of a spendthrift's purse.

My sheets have honey-
suckled buds of him
all night, soaking up

whatever I missed.
The whole room still stinks
of his energy.

Sawing for breakfast
thick slices of him
out of the seasoned air

I've no intention of
opening the window
or scrubbing my snout.

You come into my
classes an angel
in tight jeans saying

nothing – but distract
the rest of us with
your looks and the stink

of feet steamed in old
trainers: your body
sweetens our debate.

In your keeping we
suckle the maggots
disgust and desire.

The Coelacanth

I knelt to press my face
Into the muscles of his arse
As a penitent will nestle
In the pages of his missal.

Has any tongue been thrilled
At such inconsequential length
Since Adam for sheer pleasure called
The coelacanth the coelacanth?

Omphalophagy

Within an oval ante-room
to while away the interim
between two spaces of upheaval
(as if they were as cleft as *one*

and *two*) I eat the air his navel
shapes according to its own
redundancy, not to unravel
the efficient physician's knot

that would have ensured the arrival
of any parcel or the tight
comfort of a shoe, but to revel
in surge of musk and wolfing heat,

voicing into his lap a drivel
sweetened in the font of his sweat,
and with a string of adjectival
kisses to describe the ellipse

I lap and hairs my lips dishevel:
my *vor*acity overlaps
with *ver*acity, true to life
in all respects, just like a graph

(except where it's more like a novel).
I nest my tongue in flesh and fur,
calling to mind the carnivore
of recent times we call 'primeval'

to gull ourselves into approval
of ourselves and the distance we
have come since then (from wheel and hovel
to homely supersonic travel

for businessmen), and gnaw my way
down into this extinct survival
from his babyhood, to where love
is the only reason to live.

As if by forcing the retrieval
of infant warmth and drooling slangs
out of my anti-clockwise swivel
around this pivot at waist level,

I press my tongue into old songs.
Our manhood's not an end but larval:
we shuck its crust of smitten wrongs
for the raw novelty of wings.

This is the way the mind bedevils
what its need for meanings prolongs:
we can no more fly than the shovel
that mistook a sunrise for gravel.

I eat the air: let that suffice.
Confronting the world through my face
(for he is world enough) I snivel
over nothing and seem to grovel

for empty favours, purposeless
in the vagrancy of his navel.
But what great purpose would removal
from his belly serve, other than

to show how I warmed to deprival?
Would it translate my mining moan
to sound the same as now but mean
the opposite? For shaping men

my constancy suffers no rival:
you might as well deny the moon
its impetus as mess with mine.
(Besides, to stop would be uncivil.)

PART THREE

Injecting yourselves
throwing stones at stray cats
bumming cigarettes

caressing your zips
hooking sweaty arms
around each other's necks

spitting in the dust
sitting on doorsteps
lords of your sisters

singing filthy songs
in tomcat voices
invading my nights.

The brigand mountains
force an early sunset.
Under our balcony

mopeds bring Salerno
coasting down the cobbles
for gossip and ice cream.

The *bombola* boy
withdraws into his
foreskin like someone

going home who turns up
his collar and leans
into the wet wind.

A last gull scraped the
sky (a fingernail
on a blackboard) but

what darkness was due
the swift moon hoarded
in pots like mercury.

Dainty as a first
communicant, I licked
a fisherman's nipples

and my conceited spit
gleamed like the breastplate
of a marooned god.

A goatboy pissing
between roots, sweet vapour
of urine and pine,

turns to me grinning
still pissing, barefoot
in heat of wet needles,

back to his careless herd.
By way of introduction
we gossip soccer

and he goes on and on
naming English teams
as I go down on him.

In porcelain alcoves
the statues have been turned
to face the wall, their say

a silence far solider
than Neapolitan
but without the echo

of unrelated meanings.
I arrive out of breath
from missing my train.

The boy I stand next to:
his foreskin as soft
to the touch as wet silk.

He was sunbathing
on the seaward side
of the harbour wall.

Torre del Greco.
The whole gulf had caught
the scent of his genitals:

weed of the purple
sea, *calamari* and
untreated sewage.

As I started peeling
his cock he shuddered
and burst into song.

On black sand between
concrete breakwater
blocks and the railway

unsolved by footprints
in any direction
a naked Adam

or premature last man
looks up at the train
as if at a thought

passing through his mind.
How does the logic of
his body explain us?

Under where Catullus
toyed with reality
in his cushioned saloons

a decorum of very
reasonable cabins
oversees the bathers.

But we beyond the rocks,
a slippery broker
of boyhood and I

with water up trunks down
to our knees, negotiate
the space between our ages.

Arthritic olive trunk
against a fallen wall,
ants in our ankle hairs.

A breeze like impatience
on the restless lake
forces us together,

hair by the handful,
cock to cock across
the unbridgeable.

Your garlic kisses
witness me, you garland
my body with breath.

Stromboli overacts
to distract us from
the tenor of our smiles.

I and the boy in black
passing in cane fields
above the black beach

anticipate the blinding
spikes of night with which
he will coax me to bleach

his black handkerchief
and from lapping at his
nostrils catch his cold.

Bruising through damp shorts
a kilo of genitals
in his delinquent fist

the boy at the toilet door
on Milazzo station
asks what time it is,

his tone as touchy
as a wasp unfolding from
fissures in soft fruit.

He has fifteen minutes
to kill with his bare hands,
armpits like honeycomb.

Guitar and cicada
stir the green deeps
of pine and olive shade.

This net of fingers
comes apart like reason's
slow unravelling.

Embittered summer
striking flame from rock
torments a palace

already ruined,
riddled with lizards
and self-important turds.

Fall

Sicily: light through clouds like stale
    Of horses, thick air stale.

Vigilant olive trees, as lean
    As old fishermen, lean

Grimly into the coming fall.
    Within days rain must fall.

*

Conquistadors on Vespas coast
    Down to the boastful coast

Foresworn to force each day to last
    As if it were the last.

*

The lifeguard with his left hand waves
    From the edge of the waves,

Then with his right as if the left
    Had no conviction left.

(He embodies symmetry: even
    His oddity is even.)

*

Baring each armpit to the air
    With this enticing air,

He draws an errant swimmer back
    To shore, then turns his back.

*

The things that he believes become
    Him he tries to become.

A dust even purists might like
    Powders his torso like

The film of ash that Etna leaves
    On oleander leaves.

          *

To answer questions no one poses
    His voguish body poses.

Our eyes are faithful: for he leads
    Them on as if on leads.

          *

Counting the blemishes he sports
    From boyhood's reckless sports,

The humble to impress the vain
    Efface ourselves in vain

And, though eclipsed still hopeful, shadow
    Him into pine-wood shadow.

          *

As a red weft fades on the looms
    Of dusk, the lifeguard looms,

Drowsy, lacking nothing save
    A drowning man to save.

          *

Faced by his erection, as grave
    As a dictator's grave,

Within the umbrage of the pines
    A breathless angel pines

Away. The woods recruit the needless
    On hypodermic needles.

             *

From couplings all around the bay
    The boys come down to bay

Like werewolves at a red moon over
    The sea, the season over.

             *

By dawn, before the moon is ground
    To dew against the ground,

Chance is appeased at last, the die
    Is cast, the losers die.

In rags that failed to staunch its wound
    Each empty corpse is wound.

             *

Do not search where Beauty lies
    For proof of truth: he lies.

The last admirer damns him, tears
    His photo, ends in tears.

Silence

I

Silence came and sat between us
    Like an interviewer
With no questions: thoughts were few but
    Words were even fewer.

II

Giving presents to each other
    Was the speech we really
Understood: less did we love than
    Cost each other dearly.

First of May

A public holiday. Across Red Square
    They must have been parading the armour
And piping slogans in their immature
    And anti-proletarian grammar

Just as you and I climbed the Avvocata
    With our shirts tied round our waists. The hotter
We became, the more determined we were
    To make sense of our sweat by getting there,

To where majolica stations of the cross
    Defer to a view of Vesuvius,
Remote and godless with smog. Chiselled claims
    Of divine intervention in the doom

Of a weak-hearted pilgrim serve lizards
    As sun-deck: immune to all the hazards
Of sloth, they wizen nicely. As for you
    You undressed in a trice and turned on me

With your prick harrumphing like some tinpot
    General affronted by human rights
Or muddy puttees. Me, I headed straight
    For the anarchism of an armpit

To soak my smile from ear to ear in dark
    Succulence as sweaty-sweet as pawpaw
And reduce you to the unfocused torpor
    Of 'polymorphously perverse' physique.

I like to think Bakunin would approve.
    It was he who sent co-conspirators
Ciphered messages with the clues and keys
    They would need enclosed. Crazy and naïve,

But it worked: his risks travestied safety.
    It takes a deserter's nerve to undress
The undressed or to slip into mufti
    From the uniform of your one nakedness.

And were we really naked even then,
    Self-conscious on a mountaintop barer
Than I could ever be? I am no surer
    Today than then what to make of your frown

And cautionary smile, which coincide
    Just inside the limits of the lovable...
Your calves the colour of cupboards but haired
    For an ice-age of unbelievable

Kisses, the knees to be explored behind
    By any inquisitive sense worthy
Of the name, and thighs shoved apart with a
    Mere thought (like automatic doors) but inclined

To close on you almost at once, muscled
    In on my politeness and we wrestled
With a theory of love, all rictus
    Of spittle and sweat, as if with practice.

In a succession of *tableaux vivants*
    We acted out 'The People Will Never
Accept More Bombs Than Tractors' to cover
    Lust, the real meaning of our endeavour.

Gleaning dust between us – to that extent
    United with the landscape's irritant
Surface – we still managed to imagine
    Ourselves distinct from reason and region.

At times it seemed that we would levitate,
    As if, if height alone were proof of flight,
We had made ersatz wings out of the bays
    Of Salerno and Naples, and could rise

Above those baubles of the picturesque,
    The hermit's chapel, goats and olive trees
– Which were at best a distraction from risk –
    Without melting the sun. You kissed my eyes

To blind me while we measured horror
    In lengths of pleasure, our bareness barer
As if liberated by the harrow
    From shallow graves and by peace from terror.

Subverting my shyness with caresses
    That were fists in disguise, you handed out
Thrusts as swift to the fact as inspired guesses.
    How does a victorious candidate

Take and keep control? First, he gags the masses;
    Second, applies electrodes to their crotches
When they say nothing; third and last, forces
    Them to swallow and disgorge his own speeches.

You likewise muzzled me with the rigour
    Of your kisses, inhaling my clamour
– As fluent as the blindness of Homer –
    Like oxygen. According to Ortega,

'The weapon of poetry turns against
    Natural things and wounds or murders them.'
If so, this modest vendetta of rhyme
    Will make a beeline back to where we chanced

On each other's bodies and imitate
    What we were, did and became – play it out
Again as if that day had been a dry
    Run and the *Real Thing* were poetry.

To what end? Why do I need to avenge a
    Good deed? My memory is in no danger
Of letting you slip away while the sentry
    Sleeps and hitchhike back to your own country

Now that I've returned to mine. I have you
    Here: the mark of your absence from the page
Is no less convincing a sign of your
    Presence than the realistic smudge

Of mud we sculpted for the dung-beetles
　　　To investigate after we had gone.
I have you here, carved into details
　　　You made me learn by heart that afternoon,

From the adam's apple that started out
　　　As skittish as a mouse under a carpet
To the rubbery taste of your bare feet.
　　　Yours is the word, mine the tongue to shape it.

I have no claim on you, do as you please,
　　　Go back to your village and get married
To a woman you can hoodwink. But her eyes
　　　Will never leave the spot where you have buried

All but the impression of a faultless face.
　　　(For what insignia of guiltlessness
Sustain the driver of the Black Maria?
　　　The lineaments of ratified desire.)

Put on a suitably pompous expression
　　　When pragmatism understudies passion
And you spatter her insides with semen
　　　To make of fear something a little human.

You may *look* the part, but you're crazy
　　　To think she can't catch you by frisking your pulse...
You want me to write about something else?
　　　Ma io non so parlare d'altre cose,

Le altre cose son tutte noiose.
　　　You obsess me, alone now and at leisure
In the chaos of intellect, noisier
　　　Than I was when fucking you – too busy

Interpreting between our languages
　　　To say anything. (What distinguishes
The questioning policeman from the liar?
　　　The lineaments of ratified desire.)

72

Not one for freedom of expression, I
    Measure words as strictly as you are lax
With yours. I don't say love when I mean sex
    And can only with your body gone say

What I think of it, speak after the act;
    For lack of discretion, delay is my tact.
(What motivates the firing squad to fire?
    The lineaments of ratified desire.)

But I have you here. When I make a list
    Of you you come apart, rent by a lust
I reinvent at will, until the last
    Piece is cast aside, forgotten and lost:

Lips, stubble, adam's apple, collar bone,
    Shoulders, nipples – so often left unused
Like old pennies, but here uncompromised
    By the fear that beauty ill becomes a man

Unless it also functions as a weapon –
    Nipples then navel, which as if to deepen
With the sheer force of silence I lick clean,
    Saliva avid down cascading down.

My tongue abseils your pelvis on a vein
    I first caught sight of on the beach at Paestum
When loose elastic in your swimming costume
    Alerted us to where my thoughts had been

Since you first spoke to me next to the Temple
    Of Neptune; nerved by the laughter we shared,
I followed the Etruscan example
    And your arse into the oleander shade.

As I negotiate the undergrowth
    I have to keep stopping to extricate
A curl from between my teeth or underneath
    My tongue, even pure fantasy complete

With distracting detail. Our sweat deflects
    Us from the simple pursuit of our acts
By rubbing us raw with grit it collects
    Between our bellies. Its torment connects

Us even as tenderness tears us apart.
    Shall we start again? No, enough! I'm laying
Down my pen. I've had enough of both trying
    To remember and dying to forget.

Whether I invoke it or not, your ghost
    Visits me at the chillest times, displaced
From Mezzogiorno sunshine to a repressed
    Britain whose only pride is in disgust.

No need to invoke you as the rabble
    Would prefer, rendered down to a label
From the tribal babble of the Bible
    And its likes. No need to render verbal

The meanings understood in our kisses
    Or to pander to the so-called masses
For socialism's sake. Fuck the masses.
    Enough is enough. Our embraces

Had opened up a space in our voices
    For a taste of the silence that stresses
Fact, the simple truth the word defaces.
    With nothing said or left to do, our faces

Touching, one of your fingers up my arse,
    Our breath resumed its softer melody
Like a seasonal flurry of peace
    Across Red Square. A public holiday.

PART FOUR

Outside Bacon's grocery
on the corner of
Pennsylvania and 7th

two men on a doorstep
eating water melon
too close together

and leaning closer
incite passers-by
to pedestrian laughter.

Walt says to Peter:
they can have the laugh,
we have the melon.

For Your Eyes

This is a secret.
It has never been written down before.
It was smuggled here
inside the lining of an old leather suitcase.

                              A decoy
           was sent in the opposite direction
by taxi.

We closed the curtains
and sent the maid out to buy cake.
While I was making sure of the front door
you took the phone off its hook.

To maintain our anonymity we both undressed;
you were a stranger to me naked
                              as always.

By candlelight, a hand to each corner
           we unfolded the message,
           profound and optimistic but
           clouded by subsidiary clauses
           and hedged about with conditions.

We blushed with the thrill
but afterwards in bed – when we had
torn the secret in two and each eaten
his confidential half – you confessed,
you confided
                    that you didn't understand
           a word of it.
                         This is it, I said
(inscrutably)
           this is the secret.

My water-baby sweats
dilute chlorine from
armpits blond as harvest,

hot as harvesters.
Glacier on a waking
volcano, ice cream

and hot honey sauce!
He loiters on the tiled
shore of the council pool,

going pink but so chuffed
to catch me gaping at
his deliquescent navel.

Kissing would bruise, mere
threat of passion rip
the pale film of his

plausible innocence.
In the shallow of his
breathing an obstinate

pulse survives, a flicker
to touch love. But with hands
like mine hands like his

would be filleted
at a stroke. There is no
saving this delicacy.

His blushes tan the sun
till it peels. He grows
heavy in the hand.

Sheave his abundance
with eccentric knots
only the artful

sickle can decipher.
Be sure to husband his
excess with meanness:

harvest him, garner
him in armloads at
sundown, spill nothing.

Moonlight prolific
behind frosted glass,
boy in the bathroom

engrossed in greasing
his immaculate
backside, door ajar.

The clemency of
his unversed fingertips
misrepresents me:

only in his heart
can he have felt already
the pressure of my threat.

A butcher's boy, my
dervish of smalltalk
and whirling blades,

little helicopter
crash of my passion.
Imagine yourself

segmented by his
eye for a prime cut
and tenderised by those

bloody brutal fists
as he fumbles in your guts
for offal for the dog!

Boys in moonlight shine
as if some distant
planet were on fire

for their benefit,
set alight by one
with fingers to burn.

They entice the night
away from mirrors
reserved for themselves

and vandalise glass
as a star would drop
into a sea of milk.

His nose is forever
squashed up against the past,
a sweetshop window

of wanting. His brow
has sprouted antlers,
peeling velvet in pain.

After the knockout
I pretend not to see
the slow blush of his

bruises. Unwrapping
his hands is Christmas:
getting what I asked for.

You countenance my
tongue in absences
of flesh, coaxing the

elocution of
my thrust to perfect
truth to nature.

These are the songs the
goat boys sang for kisses
or a gut of wine

in quaggy combes of youth –
duets that tasted
of sweat and excrement.

Fingernails fastidious
with oil and nicotine
and nibbled to the quick

give edge to the grip
with which he calibrates
his sense of himself.

He hawks a scented
ointment of smoker's cough
into his calloused palm,

the hand as expert on
his cock as when it lights
a face with razor blades.

He stirs his cauldron
of tropical nights
on the back of a truck,

a tar-baby cowboy
constricted by serpents
tattooed through ripped jeans,

his perspiration matt
with lucky gold dust
winnowed from sunlight.

I watch him all day
while his mates are painting
our sleepless rooftops black.

He's language, chatty/
taciturn/mellifluous
/uncouth: language an

echo in the locker
room, exercised, rubbed
down. He's becoming

stronger than ever
(contrary to those
who would confound him

with crisis) yet still
making like heaven
in his sweet little toosh.

Andy

Here and again
here, I keep on
coming back to
this place, as though
I had been born

in its shadows
or wanted to
relive some dead
passion of my
youth in its heat.

It is the kind
of fastness I
could move to for
good, if not for
the snag that an

adolescent's
perineum
offers nothing
more steady than
no fixed abode.

The Blond

Imagine nothing more
fanciful than out of focus
his eyes over his book
    or from little

satin shorts to the grass
like sharp new shears his legs
clipping distances that
    are beyond me.

Heed no dream unlikelier
than the material sight of
him when, passing for the
    hundredth time, he

suddenly decides
to smile and say hello.
Ah, so surprised am I
    I don't reply!

Unnamed

What time is it? I detach myself from last night
Attentive to the whisper of a wicker chair

My unnamed visitor a shadow on the tiles
Either blowing his brains out or drying his hair.

Boy in the end bed
talking to himself
senile at nineteen

wants at most a hand
to hold when reason
threatens to return.

He will leave nothing
but a folded mattress
and unsatisfied flames.

We whose sympathy
fed on his sarcoma
will inherit all.

Hereafter

The dead porn boy is still
doing it, coming time
and again as if taken
    by surprise,

no better prepared than
the innocent he looks
for this convulsion of
    old pleasures.

From his raucous breath and
the sticky glamour of
his belly, we who watch
    him glean our

unlikely luck, compelled to
remember him each time,
oblivious, he wets our
    handkerchiefs.

In time his repertoire
of masks will seem rehearsed,
refined, impulsive as
    kabuki,

and we'll have taught ourselves
to duplicate his gestures
out of deference to the
    tradition.

But unlike the Jesus
weltering in sweat on
a gold chain across his
    collar bone,

we won't get any nearer
godliness than when he
spreads his legs and lifts his
    shaggy arse.

In the Bunkers

In the bunkers of Sodom
sheltered from the firestorm by solid salt
we endured. We had hoarded
canned goods (anything
nearer the *fois gras* end of the spectrum:
no spaghetti hoops) and survived,
cowed but defiant.
                    God is merciful.

We were not alone for long.
Filing his nails on the doorpost's *mezuzah*
but trying to hide the scar tissue on his inner arm
        where he used to be tattooed
        (an ex's phone number or some such)
the angel of the main drag
was rubbing his trousers and clicking his tongue.
        'Hey Joe,' he called, practical as ever,
        'You got plenty foreign exchange?'
        Even more to the point: 'You like my beeg feesh?'
He makes it leap like salmon up the thrust
of your reluctance.
                    When the light comes
        and he is silhouetted on the orchard wall...

He is an absence. We looked for him
at Yad va-Shem,
but no one had heard of him.

Hope

Our lips have been bruised,
we dare no longer kiss.
Why complain? All the dogs
are wagging their tails.
Isn't innocence supposed
to be austere?

This one has a kind
look in his eye, the boy
who struck the old woman.
He is taking us for a shower.

Liberation of the Homosexuals
from Dachau

Where we are going there's no place
For the honesty of the SS.
Only the body will recover.

Like seasons all the laws elapse
But one. The dawn is in eclipse
And the eclipse is clouded over.

The Descent

Between the letting go
and contact with his skull
the pebble grew bolder
like snowball or desire
till when it touched his hair
like the paternal hand
of a visiting rabbi
the chunk of Palestine
burst like a bad idea
into a schoolboy's mind.

The Art of Love and Death

1   The hunter whistles up
a premature lament
on his blow-pipe: one note
    and a monkey swoons;
the last things it misses
seeing are bullfrog cheeks
fit for a pin to pop
    like party balloons.

2   The glass-blower twirls fire
on a curtain rod, his
expertise refined at
    school in bubblegum;
while he inflates vases,
a fidgety giant tries
to hide his need for a
    pin of opium.

3   A second hunter, hot
from the kill, entertains
the lounge bar with fanfares
    on a yard of ale,
angelic on this day
of judgement, complacent
with his swag of souls
    and the fox's tail.

4   The sword-swallower's boy
passes into the crowd
with a hat, earning more
    for his arse and grace
than for the accident
itself; the ambulanceman
roots out Excalibur
    from a stony face.

5   The fifth fellates the air:
    having read in the press
    that love is as safe as
        juggling with grenades
    he does it on his own;
    in every breath semen,
    but to every dream its
        artificial AIDS.

Die in your thoughts each
morning and you will
no longer fear death.

Your unshaven smile
a matter of routine
takes my breath away.

Ear to your navel
I hear nothing but
the hunger inside.

In your hand my hand
no more mine than yours
releases itself.

Dance of the Cut-throats

They on horses got there first, reining in at the gates.
We others with our trousers rolled up to our knees
And boots under our arms were taking our time,
Pointing out exotic water plants and stopping
To photograph the birds. One of the dogs had vanished
But no one was particularly surprised or upset.

('These things happen.') He I was with turned to me grinning
When we sighted the gates, which stood wide open with
All the steaming horses tethered to them. The riders
Had prepared a fire and they welcomed us like hosts,
Relieving us of our packs and handing us clean towels
To dry our feet with. But they were holding something back:

The bad news. I was on my knees gently towelling
My friend's swollen feet when two of them, both smiling
Like doorstep missionaries with tracts to sell, broke
It to us. I swaddled the foot I was drying
And with a loose corner of towel started to rub
The calf. Neither of us thought of anything to say

Until the tearful riders shook us each by the hand
And left us in peace or what was left of it.
I said it didn't matter, he agreed with me;
'But,' he said, and explained why it did. I nodded.
The smell of woodsmoke and our self-appointed hosts'
Pounding of edible roots with makeshift pestles

Restrained us from any but the quietest despair:
We leaned together and watched the others being told.
A silence like night asserted itself. The naked
Covered up. Hands crept into hands, like dogs under threat
Of the stick, for as much symbolic protection
As the warmth of another's terror can provide.

All of us had now been told, couples by couples,
As if by pretending that the world resolves itself
Into orderly arrangements of compatible pairs
We could convince ourselves, or even crazy Nature,
That when something goes wrong there is, of necessity,
A logical solution waiting but to be deduced.

But by the time we straggled across to the rock face
To wash our hands in streaming moss, we had given up
The vanity of hopes. Too undemonstrative to grieve,
We readied ourselves as if only for food; then crouched
In dented circles, around us the slavering dogs.
The screech of spoons on army surplus billy-cans apart,

We ate without a sound, not for lack of things to say
But the better to taste the improvised meal, complete
With burnt scrapings from the pot, and to give ourselves
Time to prepare, each for him in whose eyes he thought
He saw more than the reflection of himself, words
Concise enough to make a private sense of silence.

When the time came it came early and with strangers:
Faces jostling for the view, for those at the back
Periscopes. The stamp of their eagerness raised a cloud
Of dust only the black grins of their toenails showed through.
When we fell they applauded, and the blades below their belts
Severed the sunset to the rhythm of their hips.

I took a last look at my friend. We found ourselves
Mouthing the same message, voices disengaged, the weight
Of meaning on lips alone. (The same old story.)
His eyes became liquid – no metaphor for tears
Intended – and I lost sight of him as he of me.
I could not hear if anybody made a sound.

And yet, as each last moment halved and halved again
In infinite postponement of the ultimate,
There was always something left worth cherishing:
An inch of touch, a breath, the feeblest pulse of change...
We entered whatever it was we entered
As rain a hibiscus or semen a sore throat.